A
FAR
ROCKAWAY
OF
THE
HEART

LAWRENCE FERLINGHETTI

A FAR ROCKAWAY OF THE HEART

A NEW DIRECTIONS BOOK

Book deisgn by Sylvia Frezzolini Severance
Manufactured in the United States Of America
New Directions Books are printed on acid-free paper.
First published clothbound by New Directions in 1997 and as NDP 871
    (ISBN 0-8112-1398-6) in 1998
Published simultaneously in Canada by Penguin Books Canada Limited

Library of Congress Cataloging-in Publication Data
Ferlinghetti, Lawrence.
    A far rockaway of the heart / Lawrence Ferlinghetti.
        p. cm.
    Includes index.

    I. Title.
PS3511.E557F37 1977   96–52782
811'.54—dc21   CIP

New Directions Books are published for James Laughlin
by New Directions Publishing Corporation
80 Eighth Avenue, New York 10011

for

Nancy J. Peters

and for

Allen

if he wants it

A
FAR
ROCKAWAY
OF
THE
HEART

1

Everything changes and nothing changes
Centuries end
       and all goes on
              as if nothing ever ends
As clouds still stop in mid-flight
         like dirigibles caught in cross-winds

And the fever of savage city life
              still grips the streets

But I still hear singing
        still the voices of poets
     mixed with the cry of prostitutes
              in old Mannahatta
        or Baudelaire's Paris
      birdcalls echoing
          down the alleys of history
              now renamed
And now it's the nineteen hundreds
       and the Market has crashed again
And my father drifts by in his fedora
       his eyes on the sidewalk
          a single Italian lira
            and an Indian-head penny
              in his pocket
     Bootleggers and hearses pass
          in slow motion
    A church tolls its iron bell
        mixed with the sound of car alarms
           in the year two thousand

As new suits hurry to work
in swaying skyscrapers
as newsboys still cry out
announcing the latest lunacy

And laughter arises
on the distant sea

2

Driving a cardboard automobile without a license
                at the turn of the century
        my father ran into my mother
                        on a fun-ride at Coney Island
            having spied each other eating
                    in a French boardinghouse nearby
And having decided right there and then
                    that she was for him entirely
        he followed her into
                    the playland of that evening
        where the headlong meeting
                        of their ephemeral flesh on wheels
            hurtled them forever together

And I now in the back seat
                    of their eternity
                        reaching out to embrace them

3

A native-born New Yorker
  I was from the Lower Inside
  a part of town much favored by
   addicts of the subjective
            (a subversive group always being investigated)
   as well as buddhists
    and their lower chakras
     and others seeking salvations
      from various realities
              virtual or actual
And losing track
      of where I was coming from
         with the amnesia of an immigrant
  I traveled over
      the extrovert face
        of America
But no matter where I wandered
         off the chart
I still would love to find again
        that lost locality
Where I might catch once more
      a Sunday subway for
           some Far Rockaway of the heart

4

The present is a chance event
    that stretches on and on
                into the future
And becomes it

The present is a piece of time
            a hollow arrow flying both ways
                   through the universe
      an endless happening
         with some mute rhyme or reason
    a postmodern happenstance
            performed by Joseph Beuys
    or some joker in a swallowtail coat
              and a false mustache
  or the Pope
      or some greater Happener

And flesh be grass
        that bends and dies
            in every season
Even as at this instant
        a man in striped pajamas
     comes out on
        an uptown balcony
    and drops his house key
        to an eternal woman on the sidewalk
    but the shining key misses
         her outstretched hand
   and falls through a sewer grating
  in the City of New York
        and disappears forever
          into the greater mystery

5

Where is that little fish
       I caught and left on the line
             still swimming in the still water
      under that little bridge
               by Bronx River Parkway
        when I was a boy of nine
                    meaning to return?

Swept away!

And I with it

In flood of time

6

At Ellis Island I saw her

Hair of seaweed
                    against the sun silhouetted
        not an idol in an idyll
                            but a black-and-white photo
            of an Irish Anna Livia
                            descending a gangplank
            her hair falling down
                    around a face still drawn
                                    with hunger
        in the great potato famine of 1848

And whose mother
            did she then become
                        in the wide womb of America?

7

By Brooklyn Bridge
  an elephant stands under the Elevated
    in Eric Drooker's painting
     in *Nation* magazine
      in its issue on
       The Corporatization of the World
In the jungle closing 'round it
  a puma waits with shining eyes
  as a train slides into view
    on its Elevated track
      between empty tenements
        carrying no passengers
          toward the trumpeting elephant
     who stands below with trunk upraised
      and tusks turned toward the train
      and seems not about to
          turn and run again
As a naked nymph plays a saxophone upraised
  as exotic birds flit about
    and huge jungle vines
      twine about
         the Elevated's swaying stanchions
As the sun turns tropic
      over green mansions

8

In that hinternation
that stretches Westward from Manhattan
Autumn finds the natives restless

And we pan down
skimming the landscape
as in a low-flying plane
with camera-eye zooming in

Across the iron cities
cement plains and silted rivers

Across Appalachia

Across Ohio
(first Western frontier)
And down into it

Down into middle America
hinter America
by Great Lakes yearning
by Firelands burning
in Indian Autumn
Redbrick mansions moldering
among the wooded streets
of a hundred winded towns
Under the huge sugar maples
down the canyons of dying leaves
each a hand letting go

Silos in Shiloh Ohio
Among the rust-colored trees
Holsteins by brown cornfields
(stripped in autumn harvest)

[9]

Groundswells of land
in Amish country
among the limping horse buggies
and Haunted Hayrides
in pumpkin time
And out in Indian country
'The White Man came
and taught us how
to drink black water
in the morning'
And now his car culture barrels through
Torn teepees bulldozed out
A totem or two tilted up

And in Gambier gardens
the bone-dry branches
of the famous Upsidedown Tree
rattle in the wind

As Thomas Alva Edison
born in Milan Ohio
first sees the light in New Jersey
And bosom buddy Henry Ford
moves the lightbulb's birthplace
lock stock & socket
from Menlo Park to Michigan
And drives off in a dense cloud
of unknowing
into a dubious immortality
having sown the iron seeds
of Autogeddon

9

'History is made
  of the lies of the victors'
    but you would never dream it
      from the covers of the textbooks
        nor from the way the victors are portrayed
          as super-benevolent altruists
            and lovers of the poor and downtrodden
          who never had a chance to
              rise up and write their own dubious stories
              in the mystery we call history
              (a river blurred with tears
                or a running sea
                  whose fish change color
                    when cast upon the beach)
And the feelthy rich
  get filthier or richer or whatever
    because money really doesn't 'trickle down'
    but rises like anything hot
And they keep getting more medals
  for bad behavior and for agreeing that Yes
    Justice has been done and
      the stock market is open to everyone Long live usura
      and the jury system is the best ever for
        preserving the status quota
And in fact why not have historians who
          leave blanks in their writings
            to be filled in variously
              depending on who's in power
                and the computer makes changes easy
And anyway history isn't really history
until it's rewritten
or at least until
it repeats itself
And a lot of genocides and massacres

maybe never really happened
so the record should be corrected
like the Holocaust or the rape of Cuba and Nicaragua
    or Cambodia or Timor or you name it
Even though even God can't change
a historical fact
something that's actually happened
like a rape or a kiss
But all those natives
  in all those Third and Fourth World ghettos
  really always wanted to be conquered by
    Cortez the prophesied fair-haired god
      or by Columbus the great white hope
        of Spain and/or Italy
              and stolen continents weren't really stolen
                  but were glorious Christian conquests that
                      saved those heathens from themselves
                          Onward Christian Soldiers
And on and on into the sunset
  go the histories about how
    God was always on our side anyway
      and who is more fit to write the story than
        the victors themselves who are the fittest
          having survived and arrived at the summit
            of humanity's blind history
                where the prizes are awarded to the fittest
And anyway everyone except Plato knows that
    Truth Beauty Goodness are all relative
      especially Truth as she is extolled
        in the history books Amen *oh brother*
        can you spare a dime?

10

'Only connect!'
           cried Columbus
                staring through his telescope
And he scoped it out all right
           the 'new world' as he saw it
And he saw it plain
           made of gold
              bullion and bloody Marys
And the natives 'like children'
          brought him treasures they had hoarded
             for the next Coming
                of Blondie
        (described in their *fumetti*
                their tragic comic strips)
And Johan Padan
        topside sailor
           Genovese *giovane*
             illiterate *marinero*
   crossed himself and
        dropped his pantaloons
             when he gazed upon pure flesh of Indy
                for the first time
       his old time religion
          never having prepared him
             for naked animal anima
                with no sense of sin

As nude virgins and shamen
      fell before the blunderbuss
        cavallos crashing up the beaches
             of Carib paradisos
      the gold gleaming heavy
           in the blood-red sands

[13]

And the earth shook with it
    And the earth ran with it
       And fell into the canyons
                of Wall Street Mainstreet USA

11

I would not make a pact with you

old E.P.

old master poet

caro maestro   *il miglior fabbro*

who 'gathered from the air a live tradition'

Expatriate Ezra

Confused Confucian

The Rip van Winkle of American poetry

I loved you long enough
And then unloved you long enough

For it was you who broke the new wood
the beautiful masks of your *Personae*
and lovely 'Audiart Audiart
Where thy bodice laces start'
and the glorious grandeur
of your early *Cantos*
and the caged cantos in Pisa
rising still to beauty

But then you began the broken sentences
Fit to print on marble
History's ruined echoings
A sounding palimpsest
summarizing the past by theft and allusion
(a fly's buzz carrying news)

[15]

reckoning our destinies
Polyphonic poet-oracle
mouthing Dante and Confucius
Kuan Yin and Kublai Kahn
Jefferson and John Adams
and General Washington
(father of our effrontery)
At worst an old man's mumbled jumble
of erudicities and profundities
by turns noble and incoherent
Scatter of rain on a mansard roof
mixed with antique gossip
ancient Tuscan account books
and yesterday's conversations
A garrulous gabble of
crackerbarrel colloquial
cobbled into the typography of poetry
in *canti* that couldn't possibly be sung

(But, as you let slip once
in a first draft of the first Canto
'the modern world
needs such a rag-bag
to stuff its thoughts in')

Whereas jaunty Jimmy Joyce—he also polyphonic—
in nearby triste Trieste
had already gone further in forging
'the uncreated conscience' of his race
with his blooming voice
beside the chittering waters of
withering waters of
the talking streams of consciousness
i fiumi della nostra vita

And it was you then
who stoked the wood

[16]

into the fascist flame
    in the blind world's fire
            Old radio-fascist Rip
        'Lord Ga Ga' (as the good doctor called you)
Furbo Musso-phile
        who gave the fascist salute to friends
                mouthing off on Radio Roma
                        and in vain Venezia
                    (like D'Annunzio courting Il Duce
                before *fascismo* became *fascista*)
So they took you in
the conquerors in khaki
The *americani* took you in
as a traitor or a space-case
And threw you in that cage in Pisa
And took your rage back to America

And you then strolling
in Saint Elizabeth's mental gardens
(sad the long waste years
of blasted genius!)
Until at last released—
Old Rip himself   ·
        sprung from the Catskills of his own deep slumber
        (having not read or rolled the psychedelic papers
                of the new consciousness)
Then split straightaway back to the Old World
the crenelated camembert of Olde Europa

And there in your Venetian dotage
heated up the old pottage
and mumbled a form of repentance
that Jews were your
'stupid suburban prejudice'
but stopped short there
                baffled into silence!

      your *lume* truly *spento*

A *blown husk that was finished*
                              but the light sang eternal

And the enormous dream
still in your eyes
having beaten out your exile

#12

And Pablo Neruda
       that Chilean omnivore of poetry
     who wanted to
          put everything in
            and take nothing out
               (of his *Canto General*)
   said to me in Havana Libre Hilton 1959
              'I love your wide open poetry'
     by which he meant a certain kind of
        poesía norteamericana
           and its rebel band who
        rose over the rooftops of
            tenement boneyards
        intent on making out

And made out of madness
       a hundred years of beatitude

'So boring I'm snoring'
       cried Joe Public
     before *they* came along
    and busted out the sides
          of *Poetry* Chicago
    and various New Yorkerish
          poetasters
       out of their Westchester cradles
             endlessly rocking
        on the Times Square Shuttle
      between the *Times Book Review*
         and the Algonquin
    while lady critics and gent professors
         moaned about poetic pederasts
            at Columbia

They cruised Times Square and America
                              and cruised into history
                                   'waving genitals and manuscripts'
And tuned their holy unholy voices
                         to a wide open society
                                        that didn't yet exist
And so jump-started
                    the stalled merry-go-round
                                             of American ecstasy
                              left along East River's
                                        echoing shores
                         after Old Walt stepped off
                                        Brooklyn Ferry
                                        into the heart of America

#13

Whereas Einstein was not the James Joyce of scientists and James Joyce was not the Einstein of novelists who no one could go beyond because beyond was a space where all is curved and comes around again to its beginning in a relative sort of way and after all isn't that what a river does always turning back upon itself like a serpent eating its tail which is life itself and everyone's life like a rushing stream down a mountain into the greatest river and the river always coming back to itself after it flows to the ocean and returns in clouds and rain and sunsets although today sunsets are dying the rivers dying and how much longer will the river be returning and returning as if a river really ever could come home again with its voyagers and that far wanderer James Joyce always leaning back to listen to old River Liffey telling him the great tale always whispering to him that wake of words for all of us to wail upon along a riverrun homing in the gloaming

influences + theories

14

The defeated Romanticism
  of T. S. Eliot
        and his pathetic phallusies
                    haunted my schooldays
He would not go away
His spent phrases
      dripped in my inner ear
                whenever a poet was near
Everyone echoed him
            even Anglican preachers
A defrocked Prufrock
  and his exhausted libido
    stalked my boys' school hallways
        hand in hand with
          Mister Quichotte
              the young English tutor
                (He wore his trousers rolled)
Only old Graves
    in First Year Latin
        would not bow down
              sticking to his Juvenal
                and the Bucolics
We were sure at night he tippled
            with Dionysus
And flung off his Harris tweed and
        mounted the lovely housemaid
                in Honors Cottage
    And heard the mermaids singing
              each to each
            And heard them singing to himself
And off and on made faces at
        a copy of *The Waste Land*
              on a very high shelf

15

And Samuel Beckett's house of cards
    made of silence
        of the pure speech of silence
    the silence between our words
           or others' words and ours
   or the speech we all speak
          upon dying
And Beckett with his silences
    even when young & Irish
       began making his way underground
               toward the total silence of death
It was as if his whole life
        were an end-game
             headed underground
And with Nagg and Nell and Hamm and Clove
          he sank deeper and deeper
And with Krapp he made his Last Tape
          on the way down
And Murphy became Molloy
      and Molloy became Malone
         And Malone died talking
       but his brain continued turning over
              underground
And still much later could be heard
        mutterings
        moanings
           disjointed curses
              baby mouthings
                 last gasps
   the last gasps of
      his muted consciousness
        that in spite of all that fall
          fain would not leave us

16

So that
    the God whom humans had decided
    is Consciousness itself
    whose center is the self
    and its circumference
        everywhere
looked down from the outskirts
    of His empire of the conscious
      in the far suburbs of His kingdom
where He had set up
    a temporary headquarters
    a sort of summer pavilion
    or rather a winter palace
  since it was quite cold
    way out there in space & time
       and much warmer
       down in the heart & mind of things

And He looked down from His throne
  which was of the portable variety
    sort of like a Port-O-Let
    with handles fore-and-aft
    so that He could be carried
       anywhere as needed
    without dismounting
because He was always having to move
      on the run
     depending upon
    where His Beings
    human and inhuman
      had shifted their consciousness
    which was constantly expanding
     by natural or non-natural means

So that
      He looked down from His high throne
                  and saw light upon the face of the earth
                              and saw that it was good
And He said to Himself looking down
                        'It's a good deal!
                              Life is a good deal!'
            although even as He spake it
                  He could hear a devilish voice
                  behind him whispering
                                    'Life sucks'
            which was very discouraging to God
            who would go into these
                              deep glooms
            (and some suspected
                        he was a manic depressive)
But He
      would always manage to
                        climb up and out
      where He could see
                  the light on earth again
So that He looked down again
            just this past winter and
                  decide to take a New Year's inventory
            and took out his portable Mac
                        and started to write down everything
            such as:

One Dutch ship sighting Sandy Hook New Jersey
            and mistaking it for
                        the Hook of Holland
One very beautiful woman
            weeping in a restaurant
                  her hand held
                        by a black lover
One red lobster on a leash
            strolling down a Paris boulevard

One very small dog peeing
        on a very large tree
           in which two birds are
                trying to sing
One roar of an MGM lion
              on a silver screen
One fine day under the Linden trees
           in Boston Common
One ice cream cone about to be licked
              by a boy in short pants
One enlightened politician
           behind bars
One Zapatista
And one fine anarchist picnic
And one monkey playing a masterpiece
                  on a computer
One merry-go-round on a deserted playground
      with wooden horses all galloping
        in the same direction
One spent serpent eating its own tail
One cool evening in autumn capitals
           their avenues of leaves ablaze
One Prague symphony written on
             the walls of Auschwitz
And a stone a leaf an unfound door
And a cow a clod a far figure
      by a railroad crossing at dusk
        to flash upon a Pullman window
              and be gone
And the great cracked bell of St. Sulpice
              shaking the dusk of Paris
And Mother in a manger
    because no room at an inn
And a kid called Jesus
        posing as a Christchild

And a flight of blackbirds
over the Appian Way
where legions in battle dress
are once again marching
And one hot soccer star
wearing a Forza Italia armband
And six hundred and forty-three delegates
to an over-population conference
walking out on the Pope
who refuses to wear a condom

And one egg
rolling under a pushcart
pursued by three billion people
And one moment of silence
And one moment of epiphany
One moment of ecstasy
One moment of madness
And one moment of silence

And still looking down at everything
God spake in tongues and said:
'Ah yes
and these are all thoughts I acted out
but they were only tryouts for
the real thing'

And hence He started to sing
in his *vox populi*
a whole new opera
(all of which turned out to be
the libretto for
our twenty-first century)
with a singing part for every heart
and even a part
for the very heart
of our ungodly
unconscious

17

Do dreams rescue your ego
            as an ocean saves a sinking ship?
Things you cannot deal with
      in waking life
        like an iceberg off the bow
           are transformed in dreams
             to something you
               can throw a lifeline to
                   or recognize as some pale idol
                   or familiar monster
                     whom you have already
                        learned to deal with
     like some old friend or lover
       still coming around
         for free kisses
           or other doubtful blisses

So that you wake with some elation
        and instead of the torments of
                      the great hereunder
         you hear again the ego's
                erotic thunder

And await the lightning's
         next illumination

#18

Narcissus always carried
        a small hand mirror
                just in case there was no water
     to see the self in
            like most of the rest of humanity
               carrying their little vanities
And the child
     for the first time seeing
              a shell of the self
            (and shocked by the sight of it)
Spends the rest of life enslaved
     to this so-true-and-false
                mirror image
   and only now and then seeing
          over a shoulder
             the world beyond the mirror
    and never reflecting
        that life itself
           be only a samsara illusion
  in the hand-held mirror of
        some Higher Narcissus
      leaning over our
        little quivering pool
In which might still be reflected
              a totally Ideal Being

#19

So rent a museum
          and see yourself in mirrors—
In every room an exposition
          of a different phase in your life
with all your figures and faces
     and pictures of all the people who
          passed through you
   and all the scenes
        you passed through
    all the landscapes of living
        and longing and desiring
        and spending and getting
        and doing and dying
        and sighing and laughing and crying
          (what antic gesturing!)
And walking through the house of yourself
    you climb again to all
          the rooms of yourself
   full of the other lives & selves
        who passed through them
Rooms rooms rooms
     piled up haphazard
       in the architecture of time
And all the bodies clinging to each other
    or rushing to windows
     to break out of the room
       which they boxed themselves into
All the people of your life
     in one house in the night
        all lights lit
       like a cruise ship at sea

And you run up and down
                knocking on all the doors
        through which you hear
                all the once-familiar voices
                        laughing or sobbing or singing
And you run to the roof
        and look up to the mute night sky
            And in the wheeling template of stars
                see the faces the figures
                    of the lovely lovers who
                        had once made time stand still
            now all fixed
                        in their constellated relations
                    motionless in time

So that
        some day
            as time bends around
                            to its beginning again
                you find them all again
                            and yourself

20

When the senses awake before the mind
       And a bird sings
             in a far tree
     It is not the mind that hears it
             but an ear of what we call the soul
      which may exist
           only if we think it

And love what is love
    and heart what is heart
      if we don't think they exist
The winged petal fallen away
               will not tell us
   though it be shaped like a heart
           upsidedown and brittle as a leaf
And my book is full
        of leaves and petals picked
             before they fell apart
And they are veined and winded
         like the heart

21

O
heart
involuntary muscle

O
heart
mute lover
without a tongue
of your own

I would speak for you
whenever you
(seeing a certain someone)
feel love

22

In lock of love

lacklove forgotten

lovers lie down

and unlock the dove

of passion

each in his

or her own fashion

And all is anew

in lock of love

begotten

23

The lovers under the portico

in the first Spring rain

Held each other by the heart

Like wet green leaves

clinging together

that even in the driest weather

Would not fall apart

#24

She didn't believe
                in ecstasy
She didn't believe
                in wild flights
     that would later
                   fall to the ground
                     (without parachutes)
Yet was still a romantic
                  in her own ways
         having spent her salad days
          loving a painter who flew
              where she never cared to
                      dare to

25

An obscure composer
> she was
> but not so obscure as
>> to compose
>>> obscure musicks

She composed people instead
> into amorous clusters
> at her summer musters
>> at the old homestead

So that they fell naturally
> into each other's armatures

And no harm if yours
> was among the few
>> that fell further into
>>> the too deep grass
>>>> where swain might meet swain
>> or lad meet lad
>> or lad meet lass

And many were the swain songs
> as swan met swan
>> and ass ass

#26

He made the usual fool of himself
    with the women that night
        (as if there were still roses left
           in the garden of love)
  throwing off his striped pajamas at the
          wrong moment
     and generally putting
      the wrong emphasis
        on the wrong words
  which left him much exposed
    to the dumb winds of chance
    which in his case usually blew
      through his pants
A regular walking calamity he was
  and certainly no match
    for any carnivorous kid
     or that omnivorous
       DeKooning woman with the scythe
        who was very much into
         eating him alive
  And she did she did

foolishness
wind
power
eating

it's a comedy of errors but its obvious to me now that you can write about sex and those kinds of things w/o being vulgar or too graphic but still getting the point off across. Bc I'm not comfortable writing graphically about those types of things I realize I can st write about ma stuff and mal it believati

[38]

#27

It's a woman's world
    despite what they say
And I not one of them
    letting my male chauvinism
              hang right out
                        once in a while on purpose
Like barking up a tree
      in which a siren cat
         has taken refuge
            from a dog's world
     stretched out up there
            hidden among the leaves
        languourous
           enigmatic
       long-haired and
          sinuous as a lynx

And totally in control of the situation

#28

I heard a woman making love today
                              to some beast
Through the wall I heard her voice cry out
                                   in ecstasy
                              or pain or joy
                              at least
And it was too late
              to do anything about it
                         except go with it
                                   or doubt it
Instead I ran through the streets
                    wearing a mask
                         and singing mad songs
Then fell into a zoo
     tore off my clothes
          and sprang in among the animals
                         those adepts at loneliness
And lay down with them
                    in that unpeaceable kingdom
And fell asleep like a gypsy
                    dreaming of a lioness lover

[40]

29

And love be written on running water
                        not on the surface
                        of calm lakes

And a hummingbird writes it
                        dancing above the stream
        and disappears
                leaving only
                        the sound of its wings
While the moving water
                sings through the sluices
                                of everyday life

30

The lover leaves the house of her lover

The flower of her face

       the petals of her lips

              wound the sleeping street

And she disappears down it

        as down a funnel

           through which all life has poured

31

She came in out of the night
  Stood in the doorway wavering
               like a leaf blown
                       against a window
And fluttered past
        in the first wind

   a wine-glass leaf
         a leaf out of autumn

And fluttered away
       And wandered away

Adrift in the maze
       of her own wild life . . .

3 2

Think back through the long years

Laughter in the eucalyptus forest

And the sighs no one hears

The green lush trees still there

And the long leaves like hair

                    still streaming in the wind

And the sea's voice far off

          still sounding

              upon the breakers pounding

The earth still breathing there

Though the heart be swept bare

33

How the light
   lay on the leaves
How the light
   glinted through them

How the leaves themselves
      were light
How all creatures there
     were light
       were made of light
    the warp of light
      upon them

In the dawn of the world that year

And they
   pulsed with it
     with light of earth
  as if they
    always would be
       full of light
       made of light
Shimmering

Among the sere and yellow leaves

In the autumn of that year

#34

Light knows rain
          and how to use it
    But the rain
          knows not light
     until light hits it
          and transforms it
Just as man sleeping
          knows not light
   but is transformed in waking
          as light falls on eyelids
    trembling with dawn

And man gets up
          and puts his lenses on

35

Pure white in first light

Pure as some angel
            the canvas stood
                        before the young painter

It pulsed in waves of light

It had its own radiance

He could only sully it
            bully it
                        with his too-harsh brush
            violate it
                        with his too-phallic palette knife

He wished for a brush of fine white feathers
            (the Swan with Leda)

And he stood back

And he laid the canvas down

And lay down with it alone

And long he lay with that virgin
                        lusting for a purity his own

36

Day after day returning
                              to paint the same picture over & over
              the monster canvas implacable
                              containing every place & race
              and absorbing every strike & blow
                              like some stone-faced boxer
                                      weaving & deceiving
                              fading in & out

It is a fight to the last clout

        to find the eye of the beast unblinking
                                      inscrutable
              And *nail* it
                      And lay out its carapace

And with the open paint can
                              full of unknown alphabets
              pour or paint or print or stamp upon it
                                      a final face

37

The party hoppers
                   wolfing down the wine and cheese
       without a glance at what might be
                                    considered art
At all those Thursday evening openings
                          in San Francisco galleries
And the critics and the crickets
                        and the singles out to score
And the docents of the donor classes
                   sheathed in silk & Christian Dior
                              holding long-stemmed glasses

With the tide of tinkled voices rising

And the painter to one side apprising
                     the whole uprising
                              as if from a most distant shore
   And saying to himself Is *this*
                          what I am painting for?
No wonder then that he
                     adrift in this society
    doth drink too much
                     and roll upon the floor?

38

A cricket somewhere
        winds his watch

A swatch of sunlight
        washes across the landscape

A Van Gogh crow
        lets out a cry
            carrying night on its wing
His flying shadow
        haunts the sky

In which I
        dip my paintbrush

39

A blue-bottle fly
                alighted on my palette
  and started walking around
        my squeezed-out landscape
            the paint laid out in patches
                of mixed color
                    to match the land before me
I watched in horror as the fly
 walked right into
        the yellow-ochre of
                        that California autumn
It was fate for the fly
            whose feet stuck instantly
                        in the deep color-field
So then he began
            to flutter his wings
                        so frantically
  but he stuck fast in the golden clay
                though he tried and tried
                        to fly away
Yet still he dragged himself
                    to the edge of that flat world
And then fell off
            spinning dizzily
                    like a broken helicopter
And crashed with a terrible cry
                    inaudible to me

40

When the painter Pissarro lay dying
he looked surprised
as if he had not expected to see
so much blue
in the landscape of
his afterlife
And his eyes got wider and bluer
even though his eyes were already all blue
('Old Blue' they called him)
A crooked smile
tangled his beard
and his hand passed over it
wiping out the smile
a trace of which remained
in his surprised eyes
which remained wide open
as life left him
like windows on the endless landscape
inside him
which he had all his life
been painting

41

By the statue of Rodin
> I sat down and wept

This metal cast from his clay
> the living clay
>> in his image
>>> Come to this!

How could it die
> his genius clay
>> fall into nothingness

dissolve in earth and sky
>> disappear from us

Seer who saw with his fingers
> Felt all
>> with his hands

Maestro maker and imaginer
> realist supreme

life lover and death defier
>> Eros eternal

Molding heads
> with one hand
>> out of our dust

breathing life into it
> Great clay images
>> of us

(heroic and pathetic!)
>> breathing life eternal

How then himself
> his own clay body
>> fallen apart

rotted down
> to dust

and resurrected here
> in metal effigy?
>> *Ah Rodin—Rodin!*

42

In the catalog raisonné
                of Hieronymus Bosch
    the medieval imagination
                struggles up
                    through the dank Dark Ages
                    with its hallucinations and live chimeras
                    and its horrible fear of Hell
As Bosch himself sloshes through
                        the visionary swamps of his painting
            wielding a wicked paintbrush
            loaded with the first liquid light
            of the first dawn seen
                        since the diamond light of Greece
        with which he painted the first crack
        in the sky of the medieval night
        through which then poured
        his fantastic horde of
            heretic erotics
            platonic ecstatics
            pagan ascetics
            anarchist alchemists
        singing sibyls and libertine layabouts
            angels and monks and animals
            doing heavenly things to each other
            in Rube Goldberg chains of being
            in paradisos and purgatorios
            of their own making—
            all 'Brothers & Sisters of the Free Spirit'
            a secret heretic cult
            to which Bosch himself belonged
                and for whom he painted
                    his hidden heresies
    (while all the while doing straight jobs
                            for the Church)

[54]

And the illuminati of
        this <u>counterculture cult</u>
                in secret underground rites
                        acting out their reincarnations of love
                                in the spaced-out spirit of the Holy Ghost
                                    exalted to a state of spiritual perfection
                                        and immune from Sin
                                            even in flesh on earth
                                as if they had found a way
                                        back into a permanent Paradise
                where they now lived and loved
                                in the purest state of erotic innocence

And that only the beginning
            of the supra-sensual liberation
                                    of enslaved true believers
                                        enchained for centuries
                with El Bosco and his brush depicting
                    a lady serpent in a tree
                    offering a new apple to
                            a reconstituted Adam & Eve
                                <u>(with Eve taller than Adam)</u>
Only this time around
                            they are incorruptible
                having learned from their primeval therapists
                that they didn't *have* to accept
                            the shame of Original Sin
                which their old guilt-driven religion
                            was still laying on them
And Bosch further depicting
            a whole phantasmagoria of pure extasis
                    in the first garden of divine delight
                        in which Adam was the original hairy man
                        and Eve as glabrous as light itself
                            on the First Morning redawning
And flesh was grass
                    (and living beings all leaves of grass)

in a great 'Hay Wagon' of God's Harvest
           with its myriad liberated lovers
                        (woman and man and animal)
And Seven Deadly Sins hung out to dry
           with their too lively sons
And a Ship of Fools in flames
        beyond which floats a thatched church
           with a woman's head for a roof
                and a naked maid in its open door
                near a prone dreamer
                    with a lizard for penis

And Death with a spear
              behind an uncertain curtain
And a nude nun beating the bare buns
        of a bent-over blond
      while an avid pig in nun's clothing
                embraces a pavid parishioner
And an armored animal with human legs
    mounts a man stretched out
        on the strings of a harp
              as a hidden hand fingers a vulva
            and beats the bung of a drum
                from which music notes are strung
And a horny unicorn drinks
      from a fountain of couth youth
And an Avenging Angel with sword upraised
    chases a terrified Adam & Eve
              into a dark wood
While multi-cultural couples disport
          in heavenly hot springs
             with birds and apples on their heads
        and bathers on nude beaches by blue lakes
                  cling together kissing
                   with mouths missing
                   but tongues entwined

While out of a deep
                egg-shaped pond
                        all kinds of retro creatures crawl
                                toward the golden light of day
As a flight of flapping Jurassic monsters
        pours through a futurist sculpture
                mounted on a fertile turtle
Beyond which waits a knight in fish-scale armor

And the scales weighing everything
                                in that Garden of Earthly Delights
                in which El Bosco saw
                                not the Natural History of Evil
        where all would burn forever for their sins
                as the True Church chose to see it
        but the real world as he saw it
                a derisive allegory
                                of libidinous life on present earth
        as if Evil were really nothing but
                                a tragicomic side-effect
        and his paintings actually
                the secret psychedelic posters for
                        the liberated orgies of his time

mythology → medieval times
→ religion → sacrilege.
He has a very
    "what if?"
        mentality
            here.
    Followed by what he
thinks would happen.

[57]

43

In the Beginning
                    wasn't the Word
   since we name an image
                         after we see it
As for instance when
               that time
                    before the beginning of rhyme
When Adam one morning
                  went out wordless
            into the gloaming
                    of his early morning Garden
And speechless saw
              for the first time
                  the sun rise radiant
                        over the rim of the world
And then burst out
             with an inchoate sound of ecstasy
                    a wordless mantra to the sun
And he had no word for it
         until much later he bit
            into the big apple of knowledge
            with its wondrous
                    pips of words

44

Reaching into the great abyss
$\qquad$ of the world's long night
And presuming that in the Beginning
$\qquad$ was Darkness
$\qquad$ and Light just the afterglow
$\qquad$ of a red shift
The poet
$\qquad$ fathoming the unknown
$\qquad$ like a deep ocean trawler
$\qquad$ drags for primal images
$\qquad$ with gillnet wordnets out to catch
$\qquad$ the last wild *lingua franca*
$\qquad$ the blind fish of man's fate

45

Oh you gatherer
    of the fine ash of poetry
        ash of the too-white flame
            of poetry

Consider those who have burned before you
        in the so-white fire

Crucible of Keats and Campana
    Bruno and Sappho
        Rimbaud and Poe and Corso
   And Shelley burning on the beach
        at Viarreggio

And now in the night
    in the general conflagration
      the white light
        still consuming us
     small clowns
      with our little tapers
        held to the flame

46

And every poem and every picture
                     a sensation in the eye and heart
Something that jolts you awake
           from the rapt sleep of living
       in a flash of pure epiphany
             where all stands still
                   in a diamond light
    transfixed
         revealed
            for what it truly is
                  in all its mystery
So a bird is an animal
         flown into a tree
               singing inscrutable melodies
As a lover stands transparent
        screened against the sun
            smiling darkly in the blinding light

47

In far-out poetry
>
> the heart bleeds upon the page
>> shamelessly
>
> as printer's ink bleeds onto
>> the fine tooth of paper

As blood in its rage
>
> beats through the body
>> blind in its courses

Leaving its indelible imprints
>
> those fine tattoos of living
>> known as poems

48

O fragile poems
> flowers of night-love

Quivering of guitars
> by the Guadalquivir

Echoed voices
> on sunlit terraces

White statues on bridgeheads
> And 'the white arms of roads'

Leap of wild horses
> pawing the earth

Trains in the night
> their haunted whistles hid
>> in book of time

Autumn evenings on Third Avenue
> the ochre light falling

Dressmakers' dummies undressed
> on tenement fire escapes

Newborn babies thrust
> into baths of tears

Laughter like crystal shattering
> Champagne glasses thrown
>> against fireplaces

Dawn and the exhausted lovers
> still to be sated—

All, all poems in the human dream
> still to be liberated!

49

Never a madman
Yet never far
from ludic laughter
A stand-up tragedian
I'd still absurdly ask the ultimate
of art and poetry
Only the absolute need apply
(ah hypocrite postmodern, pass by!) ‾extremes!!!
Bare beauty
like a rock statue in an ocean
above the waves unbreachable
The Goddess bald
or the Godhead shaven
seen full-on
Let them turn toward us
gesturing
insurgent
And shake the world
shake our senses
sensors and censors
Let the walls of the temple shake
and concrete cities crumble
Let the stars shine through
A hole in heaven
(as through the dome of the Pantheon)
to see the ultimate
white night
the final
antic vision

#50

The mind dances
        when the body lets it

And when the body cannot
        the mind dances within

But sometimes they move together
        and together sway
        and fly together
        and dance and sing

And then it is indeed
        an enchanting thing

51

The dance of the mind
    through Mozart's wind concertos
        with only one part of the flashing brain

                illuminated at any one time
And then at the very ending
              as at the climax of a Living Theatre play

  the whole astounding head
              seen for the first time
   the movements turning together

              as inside a crystal clock
        enmeshed in a great crescendo
                as if all the piercing insights

    of an impassioned lifetime
              now sang together in one great
        lyric breakthrough
              into inner space

52

The leaves danced to Mozart
                    above the world's static

It was an art they could understand

It was as if
        some god were listening
                    through them
    and dancing with them
               ecstatic

53

Death comes on
                    like a Beethoven concerto
            the composer himself on the stand
                    both arms extended
                    to his own skies
            the deep heaven of his orchestra
        driven to escape that absolute silence
            which he knows will come
                with the last movement

And he raises his shaggy mane
                            and shakes his hoary locks
And all falls
            deafening
                    upon him
                            in the final unheard chord

54

I wring the neck of the swan
      the horn of the old-fashioned
            wind-up phonograph
I wring the neck of nostalgia
        but the throaty voice
            keeps coming out
                eternal

      in that smokey jazz *cave*
          under the Deux Magots
             Saint Germain midnight

And Piaf singing
        in her Parigot argot
             Je ne regrette rien
             Je ne regrrrette rrrrien . . .
The orphan's eyes
        the black short dress
         the huskless voice
           made of smoke and Pernod

The mask of her face
      fallen out of darkness

55

The cat doing kundalini

arches his back and

stretches up

doing the Flight of the Swan

with Leda looking on

56

A very large cat ate a singing bird
And the cat digested the birdsong
and started singing and
then a very large dog came along
and heard the cat singing
and said to himself
If only I could sing like that
And so the dog ate the cat
and the dog started singing
and a ferocious wild lion
who just happened to be in the neighborhood
heard the dog singing like a bird
and said to himself If only I could sing like that
my old lady might let me back into
her nice warm cave
and so the lion ate the singing dog
and sure enough the lion
started singing very sweetly
(if a bit extra loud)
And then a postmodern man came along
and heard the lion singing
where he lay rolling in the grass
and the man said to himself
This is what we have all lost and
if I eat the singing lion perhaps
we can get it all back
including my mind
And so the man ate the lion and then
the man started singing
as if pure lyricism
hadn't been banned
in the postmodern world
And pretty soon all the men & women on earth
started singing together

(if a bit off-key)
and their music reached to the skies
a very fine musick indeed
But then one fine day
the universe swallowed the world whole
and the whole universe
like one sentient being
fell into a new perfect harmony
And it was the true music of the spheres
a visionary music
                a slow music
 an andante music
                  a singing in the inner ear

57

The Italian-American bimbo from Brooklyn
   assured me we had
      the best seats on the plane
And indeed they were
  except for the First Class passengers
        up front
   who lay back like
      they would get there
        long before us
    or were about to
      fly to heaven
   having been provided with
     tiny little sets of silver wings
      which they waved languidly
   between sips of champagne and caviar
      and all the while smiling sweetly
        at each other
  as if they never had killed
      their first mates
   with daggers in their eyes
     nor had ever said
       a mean word to anyone
    in all their beautiful lives

And all the rest of us
    just sitting there
      row on row as evermore
   with our boxed lunches
  and our bare faces hanging out
    looking just like proles
      in Orwell's woeful *1984*

#58

The plane wings away toward heaven
and an angel's multilingual voice
                              comes over the headphones
                  sensual as Sappho
                      (ah why is the erotic
                                      so despotic?)
And it's Italian opera all the way
                              across gigantic Atlantic
        with these flying orchestras—
                              How they soar!
            Forty thousand feet is nothing
                          in this stratosphere of
                          Verdi   Puccini   Rossini
And it's still unreal
                    this winged metal creature hurtling
            through the dark air
            airplane heir to Icarus
                    lighted eyes curtained
                              into the red dawn
                  over old Europa
                              which we swoop over now
                  like Ruskin's eagle
                              over the Apennines

What white cliffs What grey headlands!

Ah but they are only clouds
                    alto cumulus
                              towering up

And there's the sea again
                                        Mare mediterraneo
                        Old ships still
                                                set forth on it
            Columbus
                        sets out his signal flags

As we come floating in

59

The vast port sways with creaking cordage
Lost among outcries of evening
and the million eyes of autos
in the resounding city—

Lush Sicilian madonna
                        with lip-hung cigarette
Flesh octopus with raucous laugh
      hangs out a glassless window
                  in the dark cave of
                           a Genovese alley
A debased heat flows
from the iron arms of the city
flooding up through flesh
                        to the rouged nipples

And myriad men in the eternal night
                with limp cocks and unfed hearts
                      stagger away
                              through the centuries

60

Roma	Rome
La pioggia	Rain
sul Tevere	on the Tiber
Le foglie	Leaves
cadono	fall
come	like
gocce	raindrops
E la notte	And the night
viaggia	voyages
attraverso	through
l'oscurità	the darkness

61

Roma

made of flesh and stone

madness and misery

laughter and forgetting

In the shadow of its night streets

sleeps the old dream:

Light out of night

The sun bursts forth

over the Piazza del Populo

#62

"Ooops, Pamplona!" cried the Pope
      Or "Stromboli!"
          depending how volcanic he felt
                  whenever he came
(according to the bird sitting next to Him
at the press banquet) *— British slang*
with all the other hacks gaga
to hear what we were saying
My pencil at the ready
I leaned into her and asked
"So you had the Pope for a boyfriend
before he was Pope?"
She was tiny, with a loony look
She wrote for the Vatican blatt
She had a high voice
sort of peepy and cracked
She had feathers in her bird's-nest hat
"He loved all mankind"
She sang in little bursts
"And womankind!"
"I *adored* him" she whispered
her little mouth half-open
"And whenever he came
he always cried 'Ooops, Pamplona!'
Or 'Oops, Stromboli!'
And we went swimming a lot . . . birthday suits!"
"Birthday suits," I repeated
scribbling like mad
As she fell silent
"Actually,"
she blurted out at last
"He's a secret anarchist"
as she stood up on the table
and flew away
over the rooftops. . . . *becomes reality and makes a question?*

Is she a bird or a woman?

[79]

63

Rear-guard galleries
                in the Via Margutta
Cats sunning themselves
                    on terracotta rooftops
The sun coming over

And then in the Testaccio
                  the hunger for life continues
                as elsewhere
                      only fiercer
  as wherever there are animals
                    devouring each other
        figuratively or otherwise

And far off
        lost in future time
    across the river
            very distantly
                heard and not heard
            intermittently
                (almost an echo of itself)
  an iron bell tolls
      in a clay cathedral
           ringing out the end
                  of the Christian era

64

On the stage set
    of the Piazza della Rotunda
A couple of thousand citizens
    (some still in togas)
        strolling about or
            sitting at café tables
And an old old flowerseller
        passing among the tables
      bending over young couples in jeans
        as they whisper together
        and offering them
          her so dry flowers
And they not deigning
           to notice the old crone
      with her gnarled hands
          and her fingers full of
      the thin rings of
          her former lives
     each one of them enough
          to enlighten them
        as to what love or life might be
And her lips
    almost at their ears
      in which they hear only
        the very distant roaring
          of their own futures

[handwritten: hard-hitting very sad]

65

In the *sala di pranzo*
a swarm of tourists
in their morning feeding frenzy
And then they're all swept away
into one huge tour bus
And one little table left
with one very old French couple
having their croissant breakfasts
si civilisés
and discoursing in their so refined voices
si cultivés
the old *mémère* and the old *père*
his fallen face just like his lady's
And all that's left of his virility
is his deep voice
rumbling up
sounding up from his lower depths
as if beneath the table
Eros still stirred

portrait of
ancient love.

66

Walking through the University of Bologna
                    the oldest university in the world . . .
The usual protests by unusual students
                    stoning the administration
                        for Giordano Bruno
                            or Garibaldi
                                or Pasolini
                                    or La Lotta Continua
And the usual statues under the arcades
                                        or under the trees
                        Great yellow leaves
                                    falling on them
And the gardens full of
            stone philosophers
                    oblivious
                        above it all
                            having survived their own
                                        dying fall
As I release a singing bird
from under my hat
And join the nearest demonstration
against virtual reality
led by Umberto Eco I suppose
or a wit that looks like him
                    waving a rose

67

I saw great Neptune
                    in a piazza fountain in Bologna
          with his tall trident
                    standing over four fat stone women
                                        squeezing their own breasts
          and water spouting out of them
                    into the fountain's stone pool
Only it was only
                    a huge billboard photo
                                set up where the women
                                were supposed to be
          since they were really lying down
                                inside a nearby palazzo
                    where they were being restored
                                as in some classic beauty parlor

And would the greatest beauticians
                                in all the world
          really be able to restore
                                those acid-eaten breasts
          those globes of the world
                                those ravaged images of
                                        its late fate

68

In the hills above Firenze
                    the fireflies
        in the heart of night
                        in the tall grasses
        by the tall Italian cypresses
            Tiny tiny soft sparklers
                    like the eyes of magic winged faeries
    flitting about
                silent in the soft darkness
    With tiny tissue-paper eyelids
                    they blink mutely
                                on and off
                        off and on
        in the still silence
                    of the country night

And Pasolini was mistaken
There still are fireflies
                    on earth at night
And the world
            not about to end
                        in a dearth of light

69

Kids blowing bubbles
              in front of the pizzeria
High noon *mezzogiorno*
              and the grown-ups oblivious
                  of the glorious worlds
                      contained in each bubble
        scintillating in sunlight
              blown by the newborn bambino
                          (still in his crib)
                  and stared at in dumb wonder
                                  (if not surprise)
        Worlds within worlds aglow
                  in each little floating globe
              alight in the sunshine
                  and floating away in space
                      and soundlessly exploding
                              into Nothingness
From whence this
              new kid on the block
                      did just arise

70

A mass in progress in the listing church
    of Santa Maria Madre
        in this little lost port
            on the little island of Procida
The Virgin in a glass case
    with a gold crown of stars and
        a gold halo also with stars
            behind the altar high up
      the Virgin carrying
            the dying Christ in her arms
And the priest moans in a high voice
            almost singing
        keening disconsolate
And the bent fishermen with bare heads
      and the fisher wives and widows
            with black handkerchieves on their heads
            all kneeling there
         and actually weeping
      as they stare up at
            the limp Christ
      as if he had only fainted
          or faked it
            some twenty centuries ago
And they come to save him still
        in this sailless ark of a church
            adrift in the Mediterranean

#71

Shadows of seabirds
                    skim the waves
Halcyon
        makes its nest at sea
                floats where nothing floats
    except seaweed hair
                    of the seamen's goddess
        deep sea drowned

And I too have seen it

I too have heard it
                    the voiceless keening
                            the sea's lips lapping
                    off Carrara
                            or Andraitx Puerto
                            Majorca 1950
        where the dory listed leeward
                            and the flung net
                                fished the murex up
                    drowned dark maiden
                                figlia di mare
                        upon a shard
                                of Grecian urn
                    (jettisoned in turn)

And none shall reach it now

                    aie . . . aie . . .

                        none shall hear it

                                the broken singing

#72

The long boats

sail into the night—

Farewell!

#73

Somewhere on the coast of Greece

A bride in white
  A line of people in grey and black
        on one side of a broad grey river

A curtain of tall dark trees behind them

Beyond the trees a grey scrim of sky

Bride and groom are very far apart
He raises his arm as if to wave

It is late evening

The bride and the bridegroom kneel

The river
        hardly moving
                has the slow swell of an ocean

There is a slow music
                like the swell of an ocean

Love holds its breath

In the middle of the river
                in slow motion
                        a stork suspends its step

Like all is waiting for
something to happen.
    suspense.

#74

Sewing two birds together
        since neither had sung a deep song
                in some time
Penelope thought the two white birds
            being birds of a feather
                and sharing the same tongue
      might with one tongue create
          such a strange and beautiful melody
         that Ulysses still at sea
                  would hear it
      and the wind of their song
            would carry him directly ashore
But the two birds
  needed more than one tongue
    to rejuvenate their art
    and to lure Ulysses
And the two tongue-tied birds
  in her tapestry
    could only sound a tragic droning
        reminiscent of some tyrant
            talking though a mask
So when despairing late at night
  she unraveled her tapestry
    and freed their tongues
      the birds at once burst forth
        in free speech
And the rare song carried across the sea
           to the four round corners
              of the flat earth
And the great sound reached Ulysses
      who then came cruising in

75

The isles of Greece
        the isles of Greece
                upon a wine-dark sea
I started out once
        for an isle of Greece
                    in a Wanderjahr of wandering
And never thought that I might find it
                    only in myself
      A kind of island
             made of classic clarity
   where every work of art
              and every breathing thing
      is made of radiance

And there are tragic figures on it
               gesturing
But also
     lovely creatures on it still
             about to dance and sing

76

In the gardens of the Alhambra
                     I stole a small orange and ate it
The pulp dry and bitter
          and the juice
                  (acrid as an arab driven from his land)
                        made a desert of my mouth
                            and shriveled up my tongue
                                in the Sultan's last revenge
And I fell upon the ground
                   in a deep swoon
Deep as the *duende*
               in a gypsy's keening

77

They were shooting in the plazas

They were shooting in the *calles*

of Andalusia

They were shooting on the *playas*

They were shooting by the river

Where there was none like you Manina

Manina with your longing look

Your long yellow tresses Manina

Smelling of milk and chestnuts

Among the fireflies Manina

Among the mulberry trees

Parrots shriek in the patio

The cypress trees tremble

where they came for you Manina

They heard you singing then

when they shot you down Manina

And your last loud lament

Fell into Flamenco

#78

Took the seashore road
                    and sat and watched the sea
A bird became a butterfly
                    and landed on my knee
Who was the alien
                    Whose land was it
                                    Whose sea?
She waved a wing tremulously
                    not sure of anything
                                    the whole world swaying
And I
     not sure of anything
                    agreed with everything
                                    that she was saying
As the pollen from her wings
                    flowered down on me

male cynicism like #26

79

One great bird
        flew around silently
                high up
      under the panoply of trees
                 in the great rainforest
        under the great green trees
                at nightfall

He was no raven croaking 'Nevermore' —Poe
He was no falcon
        turning and turning
                in a widening gyre
He was no phoenix
      with wings afire
He was one huge
      still wild bird
  A flying mystery
        questioning me
           and our whole world
   flying silently
      from one roost to another
           high up in his wild rookery
     where all the birds were
         suddenly still
           suddenly motionless
Only he flew about
      noiselessly
His eye on this human
       in the wood of the world

#80

And I sleeping dreamt
    of all the people of earth
                seen from a high helicopter
       And all of them as in a huge
                  round aquarium
     all swimming somewhere
          or on the bottom supine
    and others surfacing
       like dolphin leaping
         into the free air of our clime

And the dead
    the dead too were there

And did not rest

But traveled over the sea
       like gulls

81

Tonight at the great old beach hotel
under the swaying palms
the huge resort hostelry
on the white sand beach
with its elegant terraces and spouting fountains
and its stages with costumed native dancers
and its many elegant tables
with linen and silver and flickering candles
scattered on the terraces
around the oval illuminated swimming pool
with hanging lamps and candelabra
lighting white faces and bodies
flabby in flowered shirts and summer dresses
gold bracelets gleaming
and the indentured strolling mariachis
in silver-studded charros and huge sombreros
with marimbas and guitarras
and the hurrying dark waiters in white
and fireworks falling through the tropical sky
the soft air filled with soft laughter and tinkling glasses
the whole scene pulsing like a huge accordion
And I saw the whole sounding set
                fall into silence and darkness
        adobe arches and trellised terraces
                                tumbled into ruin
    table-silver rusted away
                        by the pool cracked and dry
        full of broken alabaster statues
                                dead iguanas and geckos
And myriad wooden coffins
                setting forth under sail

Over abandoned casinos
   pleasure domes and ragtime utopias
                              narco-corridas and stolen *ajidos*
All to the sound of the ocean's 'long withdrawing roar'

And I keeping watch from the far shore

destruction of
      superficiality

#82

The Spanish ants
            in their trance-dance
                        around the spilled honey
                in the Santa Barbara sun
Like last night
    at the Yoga Institute—
                Adepts at ecstasy
                        blissed-out on tofu & bean sprouts
            trance-dancing to tantric mantras
                        and the drum's wild honey
Not like now
        by the David Hockney swimming pool
                            all blue and blue azure
            in the whirlpool bath
    two retired salesmen talking
        about turning yourself into
                    'an industry-type guru' and
                    'throwing your flesh against airplanes' and
                    flying all over the country
                        in alien space capsules
                            at thirty-five thousand feet
        The airplane the ultimate loneliness
                            Strangers six abreast
    To peddle pieces of paper
                        with ciphers written on them
Between motel rooms without your wife
                            and nothing to do but drink
        and think of your own
                    zero-sum life

interesting term

83

A lion came to my window
                    and leaped in
As I ran out naked
            slamming the door of the cabin
                            and closing the window
            and looking in at the lion

He was trying on my hats
                and looking in the mirror
                                and browsing on my pot plant
After a while he lay down
                    with his feet in the air
And I ran off into the world
            without the baggage of
                            my clothes and my name
And soon developed
                a long tail
                a noble look
                and a mane
                    and a taste for MGM movies

this is really funny!!!

84

Summer passed me by

And every season
                becomes the same season

Winter or summer passes by
                        in my high flat
No one notices the leaves
                coming and going
                        and falling
                                to the cry of flutes
The neighbor must
                cut down his tree
                        to save his sidewalk

The dog sleeps by the tv
                unaware of Spring at the door
                leaves in her hair
                her breasts
                flowered with petals

And an ancient voice in the air
                singing *Primavera! Primavera!*

85

[handwritten: William Carlos Williams' influence]

So much depends upon

        the very yellow taxicab

          at six

            of a rainy morning

    lighting up a landscape

        from which we would elope

as it appears

      at a distant intersection

  the very sum

      of human hope

[handwritten: slamming postmodernism?]

86

The dog hangs his snout
                    out the auto window
Too long city-pent
                    his nose is out for wild game
His tongue hangs out
                    when he gets the scent
                    of small creatures in the underbrush
            for whom every car is a brush
                                with disaster
And the dog feels for them
                    with his so sad eyes
            but looks at them
                        through the eyes of his master

#87

The tiny little ragged mutt
                in his little plaid jacket
        leads on a leash
                    his homeless mother
            clad in the same sad plaid
                        of a tattered blanket
            in which they'd been sleeping
                            before they were rousted

And the blind wind rises

And where will he lead her
            both dumb in their traces?

They still have each other

And still there is
                light if not hope
                            in their faces

#88

doorway in the rain
a dog with three legs
with a bark and a bite
I saw a bird without a song
in flight
I saw a drunk singing like a bird
I saw the Mountains of the Morn
sweep down to the sea
I saw nudes in art school
drawing each other
I saw two lovers
beating each other
I heard a field of crickets
rubbing their legs together
in ecstasy in summer
I saw the world turning
under the sun
when day was almost done
I saw the century
stagger past in a dream
I saw time scroll on
as we surfed through it
morphing into eternity

89

I saw one of them sleeping
    huddled under cardboard
        by the Church of Saint Francis
I saw one of them
     rousted by the priest

I saw one of them squatting in bushes

I saw another staggering
     against the plateglass window
        of a firstclass restaurant

I saw one of them in a phone booth
        shaking it
I saw one with burlap feet

I saw one in a grocery store
      come out with a pint
I saw another come out
     with nothing
I saw another putting a rope
      through the loops of his pants
I saw one
  with a bird on his shoulder
I saw one of them singing
     on the steps of City Hall
        in the so cool city of love
I saw one of them trying to give
       a lady cop a hug
I saw another sleeping
     by the Brooklyn Bridge
I saw another standing
     by the Golden Gate

The view from there was great

90

Passed the Bouncer's Bar tonight
in its old leaning building
just off the Embarcadero
Lots of stiffs in there
still nursing their beers
and staring at the wall
It was that kind of place
long on atmosphere
and short on talk
Even the bartender kept silent
having long ago given up bar banter
There was no Happy Hour in here
even in the bad old days
Nothing relieved the gloom
on days like this
The swinging door
rarely swung
The bums crept in out of the sun
Only the jukebox once in a while
showed signs of life
now and then letting out late at night
an old broken moan
about a dude leaving his wife
and how she done him wrong for a song
While an old head in a corner
mumbles and sings along
And falls out into the night
with its pathless starry sky
And raises a fist
to those black heavens
And lets out a bloody cry

91

The Green Street Mortuary Marching Band
          marches right down Green Street
              and turns into Columbus Avenue
              where all the café sitters at
                    the sidewalk café tables
                        sit talking and laughing and
                          looking right through it
   as if it happened every day in
     little old wooden North Beach San Francisco
        but at the same time feeling thrilled
           by the stirring sound of the gallant marching band
          as if it were celebrating life and
                       never heard of death

And right behind it comes the open hearse
     with the closed casket and the
          big framed picture under glass propped up
          showing the patriarch who
                 has just croaked
And now all seven members of
     the Green Street Mortuary Marching Band
       with the faded gold braid on their
               beat-up captains' hats
        raise their bent axes and
        start blowing all more or less
                together and
   out comes this Onward Christian Soldiers like
      you heard it once upon a time only
          much slower with a dead beat

And now you see all the relatives behind the
       closed glass windows of the long black cars and

                  their faces are all shiny like they
                      been weeping with washcloths and
                      all super serious
                  like as if the bottom has just dropped out of
                      their private markets and
              there's the widow all in weeds, and the sister with the
bent frame and the mad brother who never got through school and
Uncle Louie with the wig and there they all are assembled together
and facing each other maybe for the first time in a long time but their
masks and public faces are all in place as they face outward behind
the traveling corpse up ahead and oompah oompah goes the band
very slow with the trombones and the tuba and the trumpets and the
big bass drum and the corpse hears nothing or everything and it's a
glorious autumn day in old North Beach if only he could have lived
to see it Only we wouldn't have had the band who half an hour later
can be seen straggling back silent along the sidewalks looking like
hungover brokendown Irish bartenders dying for a drink or a last
hurrah

92

How fragile the flesh
   how fragile the world around it
      this life on earth evanescent
             deep in samsara
How transient these
      solid ephemeral buildings
     Concrete bastions
         piled up brick & mortar
  Wooden caravansaries
       built on sand
    Crystal cities alight
       Spectral skyscrapers
         sheathed in glass
         vaulted in night
    Houses of cards
       in sleeping suburbias
    Barrios of shacks
       made of mud and chewing gum
Fiberglass cars and transient trains
      (prairie schooners into Pullmans)
         sheeted in oblivion
    Transient their tracks and stations
        their 'salles des pas perdus'

How fragile the bodies pulsing in them
         (Each a temporary shell
           housing a life)
  Ballroom dancers (husband and wife)
    statuesque secretaries
     blondes in porn videos
       heavies in heroic operas
   Bodhisattvas bathing in Ganges—

How fragile this frieze of mummers
                    this dumb show—transubstantial pageant!
    Gone in a breath—

Pale idols in the night streets
                    dance and bound to death

#93

The population explodes
    and the sun wears shades
        and clouds have trousers
And the Third World War
    will be the war against the Third World
As homeless hordes sweep the earth
    and the sun the sun
        is carried away in a cloud
And every ethnicity
    insists aloud
        on its own ethnicity
And the sun muddies and darkens
    and the old Man in the Moon
      being a negative of the sun
        hides his face in a cloud
            which carries him away
And the new Cold War
   is the war with the great god computer
      and its mantra is
        Jai Ram Jai Ram CD Rom CD Rom Jai Ram
As the whole world spins
      on internets or outernets
        in a huge mystic void
     a virtual vacuum in
       the huge picture-tube
           of the world
And its screen is swept
    with alarms and excursions
        struggle and flight
   where virtual armies clash by night

94

So show your son a sunset
                              before they're all gone
              advised an old Lefty
                          exhibiting the usual paranoia
                                                of the Left
              that has now spilled over
                              on ecologists
                              and others of their ilk
          always ranting about
              the ozone hole and
                  cancer and smoking and
                          the population of the world
                                      doubling again
                          by the year two thousand twenty
      and about how the earth
                          is coming to a sudden
                                              bad end
Whereas we all know the media and
              the oil combines and
                  the tobacco companies and
                          the industry scientists and
          the industrial perplex in general
                          are all telling us the whole bull
                                      and nothing but the bull
So no need to worry
                  'No problem'
                          as they say downtown
Even if those clouds out the window
                              look a bit strange
And the droughts all over the world
          aren't really all that bad
              because it can't happen here
                  as they used to say in the Thirties

And all those jet-streams from airlines
                    really don't spew more
                         cancerous exhaust
                              than a billion cars
And those aren't really
                    Sun Dogs in the too-brilliant sun
And sunsets are still sunsets
                    even if they are only
                              one-color sunsets
        over which pilots are reporting
                    clouds are lower than they used to be
                         before the Greenhouse years
Whereas sunsets now are more like 'heart events'
        with pollution like bad cholesterol
              jamming the arteries of the universe
              and obstructing circulation
              and causing systemic disasters

And our evening spread across the sky
                         like a patient etherised upon a table

#95

At night
      a dying star
              falls in a field afar
At dawn
      a bird
          perched above it
                  sings an obit

96

Great river

      Image of time

And every evening

        radiant alphabets

            rise over it

In which I would decipher
          Your inscrutable name

97

But what is that laughter under the hill

It's the laughter of the Marvelous
                              of the Invisible
                                        of the Absurd
Since there isn't any longer any Away
      (On the island furthest out
            there's a Club Med)
                              we seek the island inside us
                        an island in the sun
                              a wild calypso place
                                    an isle of last escape
            the land that is unconquerable
                                          that cannot be consumed
There is a passionate yearning
                        a longing for wildness
                              a love of wildness
                                    at the heart of every history

From Caliban to Gauguin
      from Rousseau's noble savage
            to Rimbaud's Drunken Boat
                        and Whitman's first barbaric yawp
From the Roanoke colonists
                  (who disappeared into the wilderness
                        leaving a note behind:
                                    'Gone to Croatan')
      to London's Call of the Wild
            to Kerouac's Cassady
                        whose hotrod was his horse
      and Ken Kesey in his bus
            with sign reading "Further"
                                    on the last frontier

It is land of heretics and witches
             runaway slaves and mountainmen
                   Burning Men and *poètes maudits*

We hear their high laughter
             We hear their high keening
                         here at the end of the world

#98

Suddenly

in the long door of night

Fireflies

99

At the Golden Gate

A single plover far at sea
          wings across the horizon

A single rower almost out of sight
              rows his skull
                    into eternity

And I take a buddha crystal in my hand
            And begin becoming pure light

#100

And are we not then in the real Paradiso not in Dante's old holy
heaven as painted by Gustav Doré whose clouds were angels but
here at this seaside Sun Festival on this far Western shore on this
new world border on this glorious Sunday morning and people grow-
ing more beautiful all the time with the rising sun painting their
upturned faces as if all time were standing still and all would live
forever and limbs and faces never wither in this moment dancing like
sibyls with the Golden Bough upraised against the sky and girls in
long white dresses dancing in the surf to the sound of flutes and
bongos as if this were the hippie Sixties once again but it isn't it's the
visionary end of our flaming century here on this far beach and
children with garlands leading ponies with flowers in their bridles
and barking dogs behind them and other wet mutts bringing sticks
and mothers in madras dresses bringing newborn babes to be bap-
tized by a very tall young long-haired shaman in feathered cape who
holds high each babe in turn and facing the sun proclaims it blessed
by great god sun and proclaims the shining name of this new arrival
on earth and proclaims its true age on earth 'Twenty days!' 'Six
days!' 'Three weeks!' and all will live forever and forever and
forever in this shining moment in our own immortal time

#101

Wearing Apollinaire's derby I am in a zeppelin with a hundred dignitaries in tailcoats from all over the world cruising about looking for a place to declare peace personal and universal Looking for a soft landing for peace on earth Gardens are sighted on the horizon and the airship veers in that direction only to discover there is no airfield and we veer off again The sky is lit with flares A man in tails with wings jumps off the Eiffel Tower thinking he's a bird He plummets straight down in front of his friends I am a boy picking petals off a sunflower in Provence It's midsummer A million crickets sound their huge drone in the night A sunflower leans in a window where I am a boy leaning out *Loulou Loulou* someone calls I have picked all the petals They fall *Loulou Loulou où est tu* It is hot in the dark room There are riots in France and Italy *The Americans killed Sacco and Vanzetti* I saw Lindbergh land The zeppelin sails on There is jazz on the wireless It's Sidney Bechet Paris 1930s the dignitaries toasting each other in champagne and American cigarettes The pilot sends a Morse code greeting to a ship at sea The band plays on The Captain sends back a round of drinks on the house sailing through the hot night an endless flight around the world We gaze out the portals of the crystal gondola at the endless stars Night reveals the cities of earth lit with leftover sun I am kneeling in short pants in a cathedral somewhere in France Christ died on Friday and rose on Sunday setting a world altitude record out of sight in an instant in the dark firmament I don't believe a word of it The wine doesn't taste like blood The dirigible soars in the summit of heaven Where will it ever land The eternal pilot pours over the charts The dawn is pointing On a lake far below the wood boats knock together Life sails on I am stretched out in a sailing-canoe in upstate New York An eagle soars in the summit of heaven An opera hat lies on a marble table in the lobby of the Paris opera High over the city a plane searches the sky making a sound like a gnat It's a plane it's a bird There is a thrill in the air We are walking down the Avenue de l'Opéra The Metro entrance yawns with its Art Nouveau mouth and swallows us The zeppelin flies on into the twenty-first century The zeppelin is life

[123]

itself The zone we fly through endless without borders without boundaries There are no more nations Migrant populations sweep the earth in search of food and shelter We throw down our champagne glasses The tv shows the endless night sky We are watching an eclipse The universe endless stretches away in endless night There must be a place where all is light Where then O Endless One in endless eternity Where now We are heavenly bodies rapt in time hurtling through bent space Flame-outs illuminate the landscape

NEW
POEMS
FROM
PICTURES
OF
THE
GONE
WORLD

This section contains eighteen new poems from the latest City Lights edition of *Pictures of the Gone World.* The numbered headings here are those of the original.

28

And each poem a picture
                 at an exhibition
           upon a blank wall
                    made of concrete chaos
              Colors
                 caught in chaos
          Sounds compounded
                  of chaos
    Meaning
          made of chaos
                'gathered from the air'
    And every poem 'a raid on the inarticulate'

And all about to fall
          poet and poem and wall and all
       back into it

29

Bicyclists among the trees by the lake

Piano music slow in the distance

The summer air is heavy
                      with   desiring

The future lover
              winds through the woods
    trailing   her   purple   scarf
                        toward her future lover
           or a girl in a long white dress
                  and a picture hat
              strolls across the lawn to Gatsby

It's all an unfinished film
           for which there is no *finis*
               (so we would like to think)
          seen through a telefoto lens
        in which the future couple
          will have future children
          in real time
         who will run through the woods
            each to his or her own future

And they reproduce themselves
         and they are mutliplied
            a trillion trillion trillion times

And the film-loop runs on
         and on and on and on
           with many a re-take

And as through the wrong end
          of a telescope
      we see the myriad antic figures
         forever disappearing
     over the far horizon

As if the quivering meat-wheel tape
       (we would like to think)
           could never break

30

A hole in a redwood tree

    through which we see

      the warp of

        time & history

As through three thousand rings

          the light sings

31

Ah there's the moon
      circling the earth
        like a halo a head
     a cynosure of celestial forces

Ah yes the moon at night
          indeed might somehow be
    on such a flight
       reflecting as it does the light
          of Great God Sun

And we down here
    blind in our courses
       still denying it
            when day is done

32

'Pale horse pale rider'

And the man on the horse
                              is Death
Across the lone prairies
                              to Tombstone
where at the Bird Cage Theater
                they are whooping it up
A deal with the Devil and
                              a soul is for sale

And so begins another tale in which
                out here on the left side of the world
                still anything can happen

And does

33

Three Wapiti elk in heartland America
    with full spread of antlers
  Racks like bare trees
        hung in the sky
 out in a meadowmarsh
    in hot dry sunlight
      above the tree line
        in Rocky Mountain Park
   the three of them
       silent and still
          and watching everything
   guarding the entrance to
         their kingdom
And further on up
     at twelve thousand feet
  only the heads and horns of
       a whole herd of elk
    visible over a ridge
      the heads all turned to us
         transfixed with the sight of us
        curious bipeds
          hung with cameras
      interlopers loping along
      on our hind legs
        with baseball caps and
          plastic tote-bags
And the benevolent and protective
      order of the elk
    watching all
      with the trepidation of
         palace guards
    knowing they are
      fatally outnumbered

34

Surfers are poets too
                    if you look at it that way
                    at least in the western part of the West
They too are looking
          for the perfect wave
                    with the perfect rhythm sublime
They too are looking for the endless light
                    at the end of the tube of time
They too would fly
          through an eye of an needle
They too are realists
          and know a killer-wave when they see one
These are not cyberpunks
                    surfing through cyberspace
They are sailors who know
                    that the sea like life has its rages
                              and can be a merciless monster
                              when it wants to
          dashing the poem of your endless summer
                    on the rimeless rocks of outrageous fortune

35

Her voice was full of Yes
                    but her ego said No
        (it was much too big
                like a sailingship with
                            too much keel
                                    never able to heel over)
        And the contradiction more
                    than any skipper
                                could handle
    Except for one sly old
            fly fisherman
                who thought he knew
                    how to bait her
                                with a light rod
                so that she'd
                        make a run for it
                                        and bite
And he hooked her good all right
        But sank straight down with her
                                    to God

36

People kept coming in and looking
                at the half-alive fish on ice
        which they could choose
             to have cooked for them

Only many turned away and
                went right out of the restaurant
            as if displeased
          by the awfully strange look
           the fish gave them
       or with the general expression of the fish
       and with the awful gestures he made
    (if you call gasping for breath a gesture)

And they not wanting really
to be that much involved
in the half-life
of a fish

37

At the Hopper house
        on the beach at Truro
I look back up at it
        on its high bluff
And I am Edward Hopper
        famous American painter
    sprawled on the hillside
        on the beach grasses
    looking back up at
        Hopper's World
    where he lived all those
        windblown years
  hardly as lonely as
     the people in his paintings
   in their all-night diners
        Sunday morning storefronts
    bare-bulb bedrooms
        lighthouses in sun
      summer evening porches
    houses by the railrooad
       Victorian façades
          of emptiness
And yet would I paint them differently now
        at the tail end of our twisted century
   as if overpopulation now
       had really overcome
        our enormous solitudes
       in which a symbol of success is still
       an isolated house
       on a hill

38

Loneliness
        is not as wildly exhilarating
     as Rimbaudian insanity
         (with bawds in Belgium
             or boys in Brooklyn)
  and not as far-out as
     chilling yourself with
        various forms of
           fancy inhalations
      or other willful
         skillful excitations
            of the senses
But it too kills the unwary
   who buy flowers from itinerant arabs
       on café terraces
    for nudes passing by
         in second floor windows
    who may or may not
       be gay or anyway
     won't even glance down
           at the clown
       waving the flowers

39

A blockage in the bowel
  causes hang-ups in dreams
    or so it sometimes seems
 as for instance when
   Sisyphus keeps trying all the time
    to roll that boulder up
   and it comes always rolling back
      down upon him
 or as when we cannot get across
     that symbolic railroad crossing
  where the train keeps bearing down on us
      all the time
  where you sit helpless at the helm
   of a wheelless
     Presidential limousine
  with fifty-one clowns in the back
  all wearing nothing but
    Stars & Stripes
  and all of them singing
    God Help America!

40

On upper Fifth Avenue
                    by Grand Army Plaza

   the dignified doorman

         with the scrambled eggs
                              on his visor

     (looking like General MacArthur
                        about to wade ashore)

Opens the door

41

In an old black & white photo
    a made-up angel
        in a highschool parade
with 'a mixture of innocence and eye-shadow'
    (the caption tells us)
        'and those uncertain wings . . .'
The uncertainty being whether
    this nymph errant
        would ever be able to
        fly through
          the uncertain weather of
    her adolescence

And I am smitten
        (by the lovebug bitten)
    as she passes on her float
        moving her wings
          ever so slightly
    Her eyes on Remote

42

She looked so good in the morning
I thought she'd had her face fixed overnight
And I murmured I'll look at you
                              instead of the dawn outside
And she
        and she
                opened her eyes so very slightly
                    that I fell into those
                                    unfathomable
                        deep blue depths
                    through which what might have been
                            the true mute image of herself
                                    very gravely looked out

43

Why don't you sometime try—

        cried the poet to the painter

  (totally turned off
            by the silence of painting)

Why don't you sometime try
         and see what you can do
                to break out of it

    Just try to show
            with your dumb brush
   Just try to show
           with your mute eye
     How the earth trembles
         as lovers after loving
               echo like bells

44

As in a play by Jean-Paul Sartre
     in which the past repeats itself
And the dice
    have already
         been thrown
The hero swims in circles
       returning & returning
And arrives at the same
         whirlpools
      and the same conclusions
  by different paths each time
Arrives at the same final choices
   by totally different arguments
   but always dictated by the same still voice
          within himself

(the road not taken always the same)

So that the same mistakes are made
        over & over
  as if by a surgeon
    whose original incisions
     were fatal from the beginning
Or the aviator
   flying routes not flown before
      not shown on any map
    falls by the same flaws
       to the same earth
    falls by the same laws
       into the same lap

Yet on the other hand
  the hero with the fatal flaws
   may find they are very much
      to his liking

and guide him lightly
at his own pace
as he sets forth upon his biking
to re-articulate in his own lingo
'the uncreated conscience' of
his far-out time and place

45

The classical masks of
                             tragedy and comedy
            superimposed
                    upon each other
               through which the poet speaks
                                  simultaneously
          make his weeping voice
                sometimes burst out
                        rapsodically
            in riotous
                    uncontrollable laughter
So that naturally
        the most Absurd
             true-life tragicomedies
                      follow after